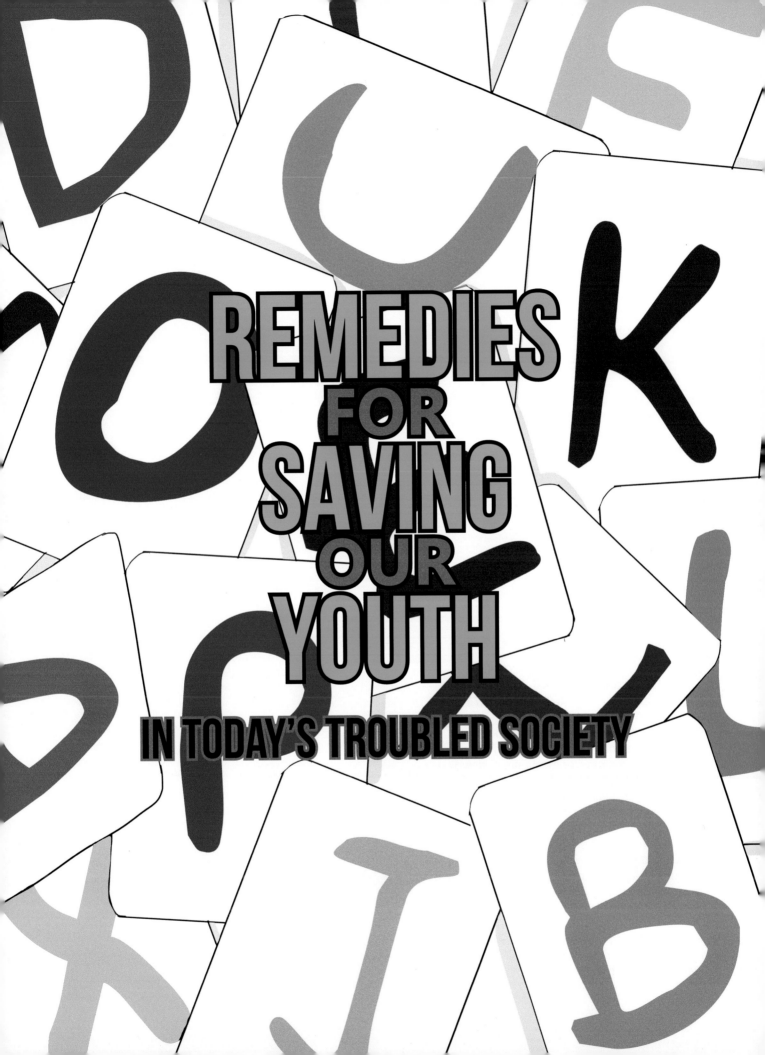

ISBN: Softcover   978-1-5245-4572-7
        Hardcover   978-1-5245-4573-4
        EBook   978-1-5245-4571-0

Print information available on the last page

Rev. date: 10/21/2016

To order additional copies of this book, contact:
Xlibris
1-888-795-4274
www.Xlibris.com
Orders@Xlibris.com

WITH LOVE
&
DEDICATION
TO ALL OF MY
MOTHERS, FATHERS,
ELDERS, AND CHILDREN
OF
HUMANITY
MAY GOD BLESS YOU ALL,
AND PEACE BE UPON YOU ALL.

ACKNOWLEDGMENTS

First and foremost, I would like to humbly submit my will to the Creator for instilling in me the intelligence and wisdom of one who has foresight to reach for those who are less fortunate.

I would like to also thank my family, especially my mom and dad who are both deceased now, for encouraging me to be myself and supporting me along the journey of life.

They have shown me character, personal development skills, leadership skills, morals, values, and respect - not just for myself, but for others as well.

I also want to thank the Church of GOD for creating in me and ongoing spirit of remembrance. Thanks to my community, where there is poverty, drugs, prostitution, gambling, murder, illiteracy, etc., for allowing me to struggle and find myself.

Even though my community didn't have the best, we always produced the best. And we always showed love towards each other, reached out and helped each other, and was kind and respectful towards one another.

For that support I would like to tell everyone tho shares similar life experiences, KEEP YOUR HEADS UP!!!! And never quit trying to excel...

Thanks to everyone for helping and supporting me to get my message out.

—Rusty Skipper

For booking information contact Rusty Skipper at <u>professorrusty35@gmail.com</u>.

Pay attention to your surroundings. If you don't strive for education and have a craving for knowledge, it will be impossible for you to keep up in such an advanced society. We have to be able to educate our kids so it will keep going as we continue to produce. Converse about your books, trade your books with your friends, take care of your books with your friends, take care of your books, and make sure that your books are based on facts, not fiction.

Read, read, and read until you understand.

You can never learn too much. The more that you read, the more that you achieve. The more that you achieve, the more that you believe.

And that is why we strive to promote the slogan

A BOOK A DAY KEEPS THE POLICE AWAY...

PURPOSE

The purpose of this book is to grasp the whole of humanity and to squeeze out all of the hatred, envy, jealousy, evil, and wickedness from within all of us and to fortify us with love and the Spirit of God with words of His wisdom and righteousness.

REMEDIES
FOR
SAVING
OUR
YOUTH

IN TODAY'S TROUBLED SOCIETY

STRONG
MEN
TEACH

We listen to certain music, but we don't pay attention to what is really being said.

When we hear what is being said, we take it and utilize every aspect of it in a negative way.

Let's try making it a habit to read everyday.

That way, it will cause you to be in possession of knowledge at all times. Without your weapons of knowledge and education, you become a handicap in a society that is as advanced as your surroundings. Pay attention to your book, because as long as you read it and cherish it, you will be productive along the way. If you drive a car, put it on the seat next to you; if you go to work, keep it near you all day long. If you take a bath, keep it with you so that you can maintain your focus.

Even if you go swimming, keep it by the pool side.

The object is not just to keep it close, but to remind you and to inspire you to read and study it. As a people, we were created by knowledge.

When you think of this worldly creation, remember that it was designed by education.

When someone designs the clothes that you wear, the car that you drive, the music that you listen to, or the watch that you are wearing, remember that they were all designed through education.

A BOOK A DAY KEEPS THE POLICE AWAY...

Brothers and Sisters,

We must become addicted to books. Not just to any books, but to those that educate you on a more conscious level. Especially when it comes to economics, psychology, science, astronomy, architects, health, etc. In todays society our livelihood indicates extinction because of our ignorance to not consume knowledge and failing to build a productive environment. We consume everything negative in order to generate negativity.

MISSION

We are the people who make up GOD's creation. To better lead the future, for those who have passed.

So now we must come together as

GOD'S children and use our love and intelligence to better our communities and to foster personal growth and develop GOD's skills.

HOW TO USE THIS BOOK AND APPLY IT TO YOUR EVERYDAY LIFE...

First and foremost, you must dedicate yourself to preparation by reading, studying, exploring, and examining its contents to the fullest extent possible.

Read it, cherish it, embrace it with affection, so that you can become closely acquainted with it. Share it with your friends.

Read it every single day until you can memorize it and recite it in the hours of the day and night.

Ask GOD to give you the strength so that you don't stumble in your words and studies.

Take your time and have patience. Believe in yourself. Read for encouragement, read for change, read for self-esteem, and make this material part of your constitution. Perfect it so it can become part of who you should be in the eyesight of GOD.

ABOUT THE AUTHOR...

Growing up in the tough streets of New Orleans' 3rd Ward Uptown District, I was raised primarily by my father, Sims D. Haley, who was a strong, aggressive, GOD fearing businessman. As for my mother, Lena N. Skipper, she was the most beautiful person in my life. She was also strong, intelligent, and full of GOD's Spirit. Unfortunately, I lost my father when I was 15 years old to a bout of pneumonia. Fifteen years later, I lost my precious mother to Breast Cancer. Through it all, I knew that it would take a lot of strength to deal with the life that was to be my future. My parents were separated by the time my father passed away. My mother left and went to Monterey, Louisiana to care for my grandmother. From there, my life began to spiral downward because of bad choices and

After the death of my father, my entire family deliberately turned their backs on me, with the exception of my mother and my aunt.

I began searching for love, support, family structure, and everything else that I had prior to my father's death. My brother, Glenn D. Skipper, had taken my father's death so hard that it led him to smoking crack-cocaine and my selling it like a fool.

This life continued on until I established myself an extended criminal history, as well as twenty-seven years and six months in the Louisiana State Penitentiary in Angola,

Louisiana.

Here is where I began to reflect, reform, and rehabilitate my entire life. I knew that I had to change, I also knew that

I would need twice the strength in order to overcome my condition. I used the strength of my mother and my father as one. Then I grabbed a hold of GOD to seal the deal.

Today, I am more GOD conscious, I am definitely more self-conscious, I am superbly intelligent, and my confidence, my choices in this new life, and my decision-making process is why I have become who I have become: a man of integrity and character who is willing to reach for the souls of those who are struggling and suffering just as I have.

I have therefore decided to dedicate my entire life to the causes of poverty, gang violence, the youth, education, and the personal growth of the children of the world.

I hereby declare myself as a Soldier of GOD and a Destroyer of Satan. Peace be upon all of the kids throughout the world, and may GOD bless you all!

Take your time and have patience. Believe in yourself. Read for encouragement, read for change, read for self-esteem, and make this material part of your constitution. Perfect it so it can become part of who you should be in the eyesight of GOD.

- Read it!

- Cherish it!

- Embrace it with affection!

- Share it!

ACKNOWLEDGMENT OF GOD

Always show respect to GOD. Try to be a reflection of His greatness, and be willing to sacrifice your good for GOD's best.

Always try to walk as if GOD is walking beside you. Be conscious of the words that you speak because you wouldn't want to insult GOD's Kingdom. Listen as if GOD was whispering clouds of paradise into your ears. Let your vision guide you towards success.

Pray every night and ask for GOD's forgiveness. Seek His comfort, patience, and perseverance.

Keep and open mind and always read from the Good Book of GOD.

THE DANGERS OF PEER PRESSURE

When dealing with peer pressure, you must be a strong leader. If you are a follower of someone or something that represents negativity, your decision-making process just might fail and lead you to making a bad decision.

Peer pressure is another word for fear, intimidation, abandonment, and attention. We do many things because of peer pressure.

But in the end, we tend to regret everything that we have done, because now we see that we not only hurt ourselves, but we also hurt our loved ones.

So the next time that someone tries to get you to use drugs, remember Peer Pressure. Even if they get you to skip school, lie, cheat, steal, or do something that you know that your parents would not approve of, think about Peer Pressure.

Peer Pressure keeps us in trouble and keeps us running.

Intelligent people do not allow Peer Pressure to make decisions for them. They always use their better judgments.

Intelligent people do not trap themselves often. If someone does not want to be your friend because of what they want you to causes Peer Pressure, then that is not your friend.

Always control your Kingdom. If you don't, someone else will.

PERSONAL GROWTH & LIFE SKILLS DEVELOPMENT

Personal growth should always be your aim in life, as well as towards life. There is a balance inside of every human being that needs attention.

You should focus on the six most important life skills of your being:

Intellectual Being - one with knowledge about self.

Physical Being - one who is of substance and material.

Social Being - one who communicates effectively.

Emotional Being - one who controls balance within self.

Productive Being - one who creates and builds.

And last but not least, the Spiritual Being - one who stays in contact with the Voice and Remembrance of GOD.

Incorporating these life skills into your habits on a daily basis will be a continuous struggle everyday. It takes hard work and dedication.

Personal Growth involves building yourself personally, so that your growth will be productive and efficient. Always protect your growth as a person because it will determine who and what you become later in life.

Acknowledge the beauty of GOD's creation and make it a pleasure to enjoy the life of a child that

GOD has given to you.

Always reverence He who has created you and nurtured you.

RESPECTING YOUR MOTHER AND FATHER

Your parents are the most important components in your life. They are who nurtured and protected you while you were in the womb.

They are your comforters, educators, and your supporters until death do you part. They will be your number one fans in everything that you do, even when what you do is wrong and you don't think that anyone is there.

PLEDGE OF ALLEGIANCE TO HUMANITY...

I pledge my allegiance to the whole of humanity. To strive in the cause of GOD Almighty. To help and embrace all of my brothers and sisters with love and affection, commitment and dedication, and the will to be a progressive people. I will uphold my pledge to the day of assembly so that through the eyes of GOD, I'll be judged by the allegiance of my pledge. I will also promise to assist those in need all the days of my life to the best of my ability.

TIPS ON MAKING SOUND DECISION AND LIVING A HEALTHY LIFE

1. Always put GOD first

2. Be an independent thinker.

3. Always try to think and be positive.

4. Treat everyone like you want to be treated.

5. Strive to be the best in everything that you do.

6. Always respect your parents, elders, and authority.

7. Make your life one of your greatest treasures.

8. Stay out of trouble.

9. Drink plenty of water and fruit juices.

10. Eat lots of fruit and vegetables.

11. Make exercise part of your everyday life.

12. Make it a habit to read everyday (books, magazines, newspapers, people, and your surroundings).

13. Stay away from junk food, candy, and soft drinks.

14. Make sure that you acknowledge GOD everyday of your life!

They should be respected, cherished, adored, and admired throughout all of the days of your life. You should listen and respect them because you're a child of GOD, and they will not tell you anything wrong.

Always listen and pay attention to what they have to say.

Never dispute with your parents or talk back to them in a sarcastic manner. Always love them and support them as they have loved and supported you.

OBEYING AUTHORITY AS WELL AS YOUR ELDERS

It has been taught throughout history to always respect those who hold positions of authority.

Always respect your elders because they are usually the leaders in your community. They are those who have seen beyond where you have been. Listen carefully to their wisdom and dance to their authority.

Bask in their intelligence and reflect on their histories.

Honor their souls and never forget what pulled them through hard times. These things will also pull you through when times get rough and you think that you can't make it

DECISIONS, CONSEQUENCES, CHOICES, AND ACTIONS

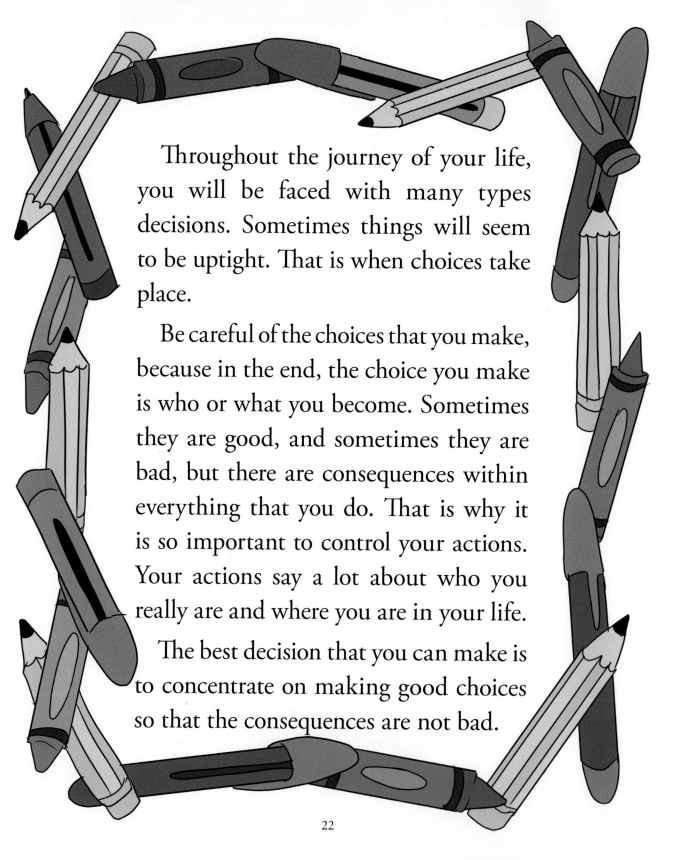

Throughout the journey of your life, you will be faced with many types decisions. Sometimes things will seem to be uptight. That is when choices take place.

Be careful of the choices that you make, because in the end, the choice you make is who or what you become. Sometimes they are good, and sometimes they are bad, but there are consequences within everything that you do. That is why it is so important to control your actions. Your actions say a lot about who you really are and where you are in your life.

The best decision that you can make is to concentrate on making good choices so that the consequences are not bad.

BELIEVE IN YOURSELF

No matter how hard times may get, or how hard trouble may seem to be, you must never give up.

Continue to strive and struggle to set yourself free. Always believe in yourself, because if you don't, nobody else will.

THE STRENGTH OF A CHILD...

The strength of a child begins with the family as it branches off into the community. We need to have strong fathers, passionate mothers, great leaders, excellent mentors, and the unity to pull our children together so we can give them the boost that they need in order to succeed in life.

The strength of a child depends on the solidarity of the family.

ALWAYS READ AND BE WILLING TO LISTEN AND LEARN

Remember, children, that reading is a fundamental process.

Read to forward your progress. Always make a good book your best friend. It will never turn its back on you. It will always be there for you and will lift you up when you are down. You can always pick it up and travel anywhere in the world for free. You can even snuggle with it. That is barely half of what you can do with a good book.

Read everyday to better your communication skills.

Reading will not only make you smart, but it will also make you happy. And, happiness is the key to a long life.

PAYING ATTENTION TO YOUR SURROUNDINGS AND MAKING POSITIVE DECISIONS

It is important to always be conscious wherever you are. You never know who could be watching.

Always think for yourself and question what doesn't seem right.

Never let anyone think for you when they can't think for themselves.

QUESTIONS THAT OUR KIDS SHOULD KNOW...

1. WHO IS GOD?
2. WHO ARE YOU?
3. WHAT IS EDUCATION?
4. WHAT DO YOU WANT TO BE WHEN YOU GROW UP?
5. WHY IS IT IMPORTANT TO ATTEND COLLEGE?
6. WHAT IS A FRIEND?
7. WHO IS SATAN?

8. WHAT IS LOVE?
9. WHAT IS AN ENEMY?
10. WHAT IS HATE?
11. WHAT IS PRAYER?
12. WHY IS OUR HISTORY IMPORTANT?
13. WHO IS RESPONSIBLE FOR YOUR ACTIONS?
14. WHAT IS MAN?
15. WHAT IS WOMAN?

ATTENDING SOME TYPE OF RELIGIOUS-BASED ORGANIZATION

Indulge yourself in faith-based programs. There should be a strong urge to establish that type of foundation.

It's good for studying, developing personal growth, establishing structure, and solidifying your moral structure as a human being.

STAYING OUT OF TROUBLE

Being kind to everyone

Staying out of trouble is not always the easy thing to do, but it is always the smartest thing.

Trouble is easy to get into but hard to get out of. Always be mindful of the company that you keep and learn how to think quick on your feet.

When you think about getting in trouble, remember this book...

BEING KIND TO EVERYONE

Everyone should be like your family when it comes to being kind.

Kindness is sweet and it comforts the soul.

So be kind to your peers and treat them as if you were dealing and talking to GOD.

Kindness will destroy your enemies and create new friends.

PRAYER FOR WHEN YOU ARE TROUBLED AND CONFUSED

God, grant me the **SERENITY** to accept the things that I cannot change, the **COURAGE** to change the things that I can, and the *Wisdom* to know the difference.

AMEN

Good, Better, Best!

Never let it rest,

until your Good

gets better

and

your better

gets best...

COMMUNICATING WITH YOUR PARENTS

Communication is the key to all successful relationships. Talk with your parents about EVERYTHING. What they don't know could possibly destroy your life.

Keep open all lines of communication with parents at all times. Never close out your parents when it comes to communication.

GETTING INVOLVED WITH COMMUNITY ACTIVITIES

Your community is your family, and your family is your support. Enjoy yourself within your community. Help to establish unity amongst each other. Work and help one another in everything that you do in life. Always stay busy and have a reason for attending the community activity.

MAKING YOUR CHARACTER COUNT

Your character will determine who you are and where you will go in life. It is very important that you develop an identity that will define who you are.

Master the arts of character by perfecting the traits of respect, responsibility, trustworthiness, caring, sharing, citizenship, and fairness.

Always strive for your best. Build motivation and strong self-esteem.

Never let anybody tell you what you cannot be.

Be upright and righteous. Also, stand strong in what you believe in. Always keep your head up.

8 STEPS TO A SUCCESSFUL RELATIONSHIP WITH GOD

1. Communication

2. Trust

3. Time

4. Commitment

5. Love

6. Respect

7. Support

8. Marriage

If followed correctly when you become an adult, this same remedy will make your life successful.

PRAYER FOR GUIDANCE AND UNDERSTANDING

Our Father, who art in
Heaven, hallowed be Thy name. Thy
Kingdom come,
Thy Will be done, on
Earth, as it is in Heaven.
Give us this day our daily bread, and
forgive us our debts as we forgive our
debtors.
Lead us not into temptation but
deliver us from evil.
For Thine is the Kingdom, and the
Power, and the Glory, forever.
AMEN

MAKING EDUCATION YOUR FIRST PRIORITY

The knowledge of self should always be your first form of education. Then comes your primary form of education - basic education. Then your secondary, which is the form of education that you learn on your own.

ALWAYS KEEP YOUR EYES ON THE PRIZE...YOUR GOALS!

BUILD TRUST AND LOVE AMONGST HUMANITY

The establishments of trust and love come by spending time and communication with your peers. It's working together, supporting one another, and striving for that one goal that defines us as the people of humanity.

So lets trust each other and let the love of GOD's children develop.

STAYING FREE OF DRUGS AND SEX

Drugs of ANY kind are very dangerous. Never let anyone tell you different. Children should not participate in any sexual activities. Sex is for adults who are mature and responsible.

Drugs are for losers. No one who is a representative of GOD is irresponsible enough to use drugs. Think about what you do before you do it.

WALKING IN THE FOOTSTEPS OF GOD...

To walk in the footsteps of GOD is to be progressive, upright, and mobile.

Be willing to always help and love your fellow brothers and sisters. Always respect and honor your mother and father.

Have faith in everything that you do. Make sure that you keep your connection and relationship with GOD as your strongest faith.

PRAYER AND REMEMBRANCE AND PERSEVERANCE

O GOD! Change my fear and my grave into love.

Have mercy on me in the name of your Great Books; and make it for me a Guide and Light and a Guidance and Mercy.

O GOD! Make me remember what of it I have forgotten; make me know if it that which I have become ignorant of;

And make me recite it in the hours of the night and day;

And make it an Argument for me O Thou Sustainer of *(ALL)* the Worlds.

AMEN

Printed in the United States
By Bookmasters